Relentless

This Book Belongs to: _____

Date Started: _____

PUBLISHED BY YM360

© 2015 by Ed Newton. All rights reserved.

Published by youthministry360 in the United States of America.

ISBN 13: 9781935832492
ISBN 10: 1935832492

No part of this publication may be reproduced, stored in a retrieval system, or transmitted in any form or by any means electronic or mechanical, including photocopy, recording, or any information storage and retrieval system now known or to be invented, without prior permission in writing from the publisher.

Any reference within this piece to Internet addresses of web sites not under the administration of youthministry360 is not to be taken as an endorsement of those web sites by youthministry360; neither does youthministry360 vouch for their content.

Unless otherwise noted, all Scripture references are taken from the HOLY BIBLE, NEW INTERNATIONAL VERSION®. Copyright © 1973, 1978, 1984 Biblica. Used by permission of Zondervan. All rights reserved.

Author: Ed Newton
Design: Upper Air Creative

Lot: [AUG19]

FOR WE CANNOT HELP SPEAKING ABOUT WHAT WE HAVE SEEN & HEARD

Acts 4:20

Contents

Getting Started —————————————— 1

Week 1

Week 1 Intro ——————————————— 3
Day 1 ——————————————————— 5
Day 2 ——————————————————— 7
Day 3 ——————————————————— 9
Day 4 ——————————————————— 11
Day 5 ——————————————————— 13
Day 6 ——————————————————— 15
Day 7 ——————————————————— 16
Week 1 Wrapping Up ————————————— 17

Week 2

Week 2 Intro ——————————————— 21
Day 1 ——————————————————— 23
Day 2 ——————————————————— 25
Day 3 ——————————————————— 27
Day 4 ——————————————————— 29
Day 5 ——————————————————— 31
Day 6 ——————————————————— 33
Day 7 ——————————————————— 34
Week 2 Wrapping Up ————————————— 35

Week 3

Week 3 Intro — 39
Day 1 — 41
Day 2 — 43
Day 3 — 45
Day 4 — 47
Day 5 — 49
Day 6 — 51
Day 7 — 52
Week 3 Wrapping Up — 53

Week 4

Week 4 Intro — 57
Day 1 — 59
Day 2 — 61
Day 3 — 63
Day 4 — 65
Day 5 — 67
Day 6 — 69
Day 7 — 70
Week 4 Wrapping Up — 71
Relentless Closing — 73

About the Author — 75

Getting Started

So here you are . . .

You're holding an interactive journal that will serve as your guide for an in-depth look at what it means to be relentless in your approach to living out your faith in Christ. This means at some point in the not-so-distant past you probably spent a weekend going through RELENTLESS with your youth group.

Maybe you thought you were done talking about the concept of what it means be relentless. Maybe you thought you had learned all there was to learn.

The truth? You're just getting started.

"Relentless" is more than a word. It's an attitude. Being relentless in your pursuit of Christ and in the living out of your faith says to the world that the goal being pursued is worth more than the pain endured. The Bible is clear that our faith in Christ will be costly. But the life Christ purchased for you on the cross cost Him everything. As His children, living out a relentless faith is the very definition of what it means to be a Christ-follower.

This book will take you on a four-week journey of going deeper into what exactly living a relentless faith looks like. Embrace this journey. Give it your best. Commit to sticking with this book until the end. It will only take a few minutes each day. And you'll find that your life will be richer as a result of spending such quality time in God's presence.

LET'S GET STARTED.
LOOK AT THE NEXT PAGE TO LEARN HOW THIS BOOK WORKS.

How This Book Works

Here are a few things you need to know to put this book to good use.

Start With This Advice
Whether you're super-committed and read your Bible each day or struggle to read a few verses a couple of times a week, the key to sticking with this through four weeks is commitment. Your routine may change, but your commitment to meet God each day has to be there. Tell yourself that whether or not you read this journal at the same time everyday, or if you read it whenever you get a few extra minutes, you'll make it a priority in your daily life.

Have Your Bible Open
Resist the urge to ignore the spots where this book will tell you to read a passage of Scripture. This book is only a guide for the Book. The close relationship with God that you want only happens by reading and doing what's in the Bible. Have it open as you go through this book.

Each Week Is Structured The Same, But Is Really Different
Each week's content works in similar ways. But, each day is different. And, there are a lot of different kinds of activities. Some will take 3-5 minutes, some 10-15. Some will ask you to look at two or three passages of Scripture; some will just ask you to think about a concept. The variety will make it easier to stick with and help you learn in different ways that are suited to you.

What If I Miss A Day of Reading? Or Three?
Don't give up! Take this at your pace! The goal is for you to grow closer to God. If you miss a day or two . . . or four . . . don't throw in the towel. Pick this book back up and start where you left off. You can do this! And by doing it, you'll show the world that God makes an incredible difference in the lives of His followers. So, hang in there! You've got this!

Well, that's what you need to know to get started! Turn the page to read the introduction to Week 1.

Week One Intro

Before starting Week 1, read this short introduction.

Let's be honest: most of us like things to be easy. If given the choice to have to work hard for something or to simply have it given to us, we'd rather have it handed to us without the hard work. If we could be in shape without working out, we'd take that option right? If you could get into a great college without the extra time spent studying, that would be pretty awesome, wouldn't it? The problem is that life doesn't work this way. And neither does our faith.

Many people who have come to know Christ have bought into a version of Christianity that doesn't cost them anything. When they encounter pain, persecution, and problems they walk away from the invitation to follow Jesus because of the challenges that present themselves when doing so. Things get hard. Times are tough. And some people think that when they committed to following Christ all their troubles would go away. Life wouldn't be hard. Life would be easy.

The issue with this is that Jesus never promises this in the Bible. In fact, Jesus told us that following Him would lead to persecution. Your challenge as a Christ-follower is to redefine the cost of following Christ in a world that hates Him and His followers. Jesus gave it all for us. What's keeping us from giving our all for Him?

Relentless is centered around one idea:

> **If you were put into a situation where you had to choose Christ, but by doing so you would lose everything, including maybe even your life, would you still do it?**

Are you willing to pursue Jesus in a way where nothing else comes first? If so, this book will give you some guidelines for how to think about living this kind of faith.

It won't be easy. But here's a secret: few things truly worth having are. Your relationship with Christ is no different.

If you're ready to get started, turn to page 5 for Week 1, Day 1.

WEEK 1 ▶ DAY 1

Read today's devotion below and answer the questions on page 6.

What does your faith cost you? In what ways does the amazing relationship you enjoy with God cause you to experience discomfort? Take a moment today and look at what it cost two of the real foundational figures of our faith.

Read Acts 16:16-34. The Gospel was spreading rapidly and the Apostle Paul was on a mission to take the Gospel to the furthest points on the earth. It was not an easy trip. Opposition from those who hated Christianity marked his journey.

In this section you just read, a different kind of opposition came from a rather peculiar place. A demon-possessed young girl actually affirmed the ministry of Paul and Silas by stating they were servants of the Most High God (Acts 16:14). Paul didn't want attention drawn to him so he cast the demon out of the girl and set her free from both the chains of Satan and the slave owner.

This didn't go so well with the slave owner. As a result, Paul and his companions were severely beaten and imprisoned. However, what Satan means for evil, God means for good. This prison was exactly where Paul and Silas needed to be. They knew it, they sensed it, they embraced it, and seized the opportunity to make much of the moment, by making much of Jesus.

I am convinced that the most secure place in the world is in the center of God's will. But while being in the center of God's will is a secure place, it isn't always a safe place. God is far more concerned about making us holy than He is in making us happy.

Paul and Silas were taken to the inner prison and guarded as if they had committed murder. This wasn't exactly three square meals, cable TV, and air conditioning. This was some of the worst possible circumstances you could possibly imagine. Not only were they trying to recover from the beatings, but to make matters worse their feet were locked in stocks. They were suffering for the Gospel.

But the point of today's devotion is found starting in verse 25. After all of this, Paul and Silas were praising God. In the midst of their great trial, they focused on the character of God and worshiped Him. The result? God was glorified. The jailer and his family stepped into a saving relationship with God. And Paul and Silas were radically used by God to further His Kingdom.

The truth is this: If you want to be able to rejoice when you have lost everything, then you have to possess something greater than what you lost.

Take a moment and think about this. This truth will inform much of what we do in this journal for the next few weeks. Use the questions below to help you think about this concept. If you want, record your thoughts in a journal or note-taking app.

Think About This . . .
- Imagine you found yourself in a situation similar to Paul and Silas.' Imagine you've lost everything because of your faith. Think about this for a second. How would you feel about this? What emotions come to mind?

- If all you had to rely on was your relationship with Jesus, is that relationship deep enough that it could sustain you? It's a tough question. Really give it some time to consider.

- Can you identify a few things you might do to deepen your relationship with Jesus? Come up with three things you could do to get closer to Jesus today.

Spend a few minutes praying to God. Listen more than you talk. See what God is trying to tell you about your relationship with Him.

WEEK 1 ▶ DAY 2

Work through the activity below to begin thinking about praise and why it is vital to living a relentless faith-life.

We're going to do something we will do often in this journal. We're going to spend another day on the same passage you looked at yesterday.

Go back and look at Acts 16:25. We're going to spend the rest of this week talking about the idea of praise. Specifically, we're going to talk about the idea of praising God in the midst of tough times.

In the middle of Paul and Silas' suffering, they began to sing praises. Now, prison and praise are probably never mentioned in the same sentence. But Paul and Silas knew that God had placed them there. This confrontation and confinement wasn't their plan, but they knew it was part of God's will for them.

They knew one of the most important things we can know: God is at work. They knew God would use their situation to bring about salvation for many of those who heard their story. Their platform was suffering, shackles, and . . . singing! They could sing praises to God in the midst of trial because they were 100% confident in who God was and how He had chosen to use them.

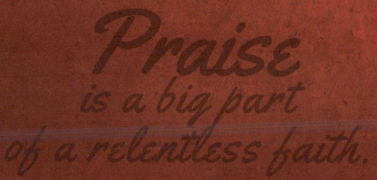

Praise is a big part of a relentless faith.

It seems counterintuitive that we would praise God when we find ourselves being treated unfairly or unjustly because of our faith. But this is exactly the picture the Bible paints, over and over again.

We're going to spend the rest of the week discussing this idea about praising God in the midst of hard times. But take a few moments today and think about what praise is and the role it plays in your life. Read the following questions. Answer them in the space provided or in a journal or note-taking app.

How would you define praise in your own words?

Can you think of a few different ways to praise God?
(HINT: Singing isn't the only way.)

When was the last time you remember spending time meaningfully praising God?

What are some of the obstacles that keep you from praising God as much or as engaged as you would want?

There's no time like the present. Take a few moments and praise God right now. Pray to Him and tell Him how awesome He is.

WEEK 1 ▸ DAY 3

Read the quote below and spend some time today thinking about it. Use the prompts on page 10 to help guide your thoughts.

"Our *values* determine our evaluations. If we value *Comfort* more than *Character* then trials will upset us.

If we *value* the material and physical more than the *Spiritual,* we will not be able to 'count it all joy.'

If we live only for the present and forget the future, then TRIALS will make us bitter not better."

- Warren Wiersbe

Use these questions to help you reflect on this quote.

1. Maybe you don't value comfort more than character, but do you get Wiersbe's point? If anything comes before your relationship with God, the trials you experience because of your faith will cause you to resent your faith. Is there anything in your life that is more important than your relationship with God? If so, what can you do about it?

2. If we value a Christ-like character, how does that lead us to see trials as something positive?

3. In essence, what Wiersbe is saying toward the end is the exact opposite of the "YOLO" mentality. How so? How does living in the moment keep you from growing a relentless faith?

WEEK 1 ▸ DAY 4

What's the difference between joy and happiness? Today's devotion will help you answer that question.

Have you ever thought about the difference between joy and happiness? Maybe you haven't. And maybe even now the difference in the two seems unimportant. But hang in there for a moment and you'll see that when it comes to relentlessly living out your faith, the distinction between the two is vital.

Joy and happiness don't mean the same thing. Not when viewed through the lens of faith. One has the ability to serve the other, but not vice versa. You see happiness is an attitude that hinges primarily on favorable circumstances. In other words, happiness depends on your surroundings. It's environmental. If life is going well, you're happy.

One the other hand, joy is an emotional state that is not dependent upon circumstances. Instead, joy comes from understanding some concrete realities: God loves us. Christ redeemed us. The Holy Spirit secures us.

Take a second and read 1 Peter 1:3-8. Peter was speaking to an audience of people who had been persecuted for their faith, and would continue to be. He had to remind them that even though they experienced hardship because of their faith, they could rejoice. Re-read verse 8. The kind of joy Peter was talking about is the kind of joy that exists regardless of circumstance. It is the joy that is found in the heart of a Christ-follower.

The endless pursuit of humanity is to seek happiness at all cost. But those who seek joy apart from Christ fail to realize that the cost is greater than they could ever afford. The new car, the new house, the new pair of jeans, the new cell phone, the new head phones . . . these create a temporary happy feeling that will eventually fade. But joy, real joy, can't be purchased. It can't lose its value. The joy that comes from the hope we have in Christ does not change with the latest fads, seasons, or popular opinions of our day.

When life gets tough, remember that your joy is found in Jesus, the same yesterday, today and forever (Hebrews 13:8).

Take a second and think about the following questions. If you want, write your answers in the space provided. Or, jot down your thoughts in a journal or note-taking app.

1. Think of some examples of times when some aspect of your surroundings made you happy.

2. Now, think of a time recently when something happened to make you unhappy.

3. Happiness is fleeting. Here one minute and gone the next. Joy is unchanging and comes from knowing and being known by Jesus. In your own words, how is this different than happiness?

4. How does knowing what joy truly is give you hope for the tough times you'll face as you live out a relentless faith?

WEEK 1 ▸ DAY 5

Are we only expected to praise God when things are good? Read today's devotion to find out.

Today we're going to bring this full-circle.

We've talked about tough times being a reality of living a relentless faith-life. We've talked about the difference in joy and happiness. And we've talked about what it means to praise God. But we haven't specifically discussed the idea of praising God in the midst of our trials and our joy.

It's an interesting thought, isn't it? Praising God in the middle of a time of persecution or heartache? Who is expected to do that?

Actually, you are. And so is every Christ-follower. Take a second and read James 1:2-3. What James says here is SO countercultural and counterintuitive. When something is countercultural that means it goes against what we observe in the world around us. When people go through tough times, you don't expect to see them rejoicing. You expect to see them complaining. Rejoicing in times of trial is a uniquely Christian thing to do. Counterintuitive means that it goes against our human nature, or common sense. It's not in our nature to praise God when times are tough. But if you've come to faith in Christ, you have God dwelling in you. This defies human nature. The Holy Spirit empowers your praise.

This is radical, world-rocking stuff here.

Do you realize that if you fully embraced this concept your life would stand out to the world around you? You would be like one of those big billboards on the Interstate, a huge sign saying

"Look at the difference Christ makes in my life"!

In the space provided below, take some time and journal your thoughts. Answer these questions:

- What keeps me from praising God during tough times?
- How can I move toward a more relentless faith by committing to praise God more no matter the circumstance?
- How will I change as a person by being more faithful in my praise of God?

WEEK 1 ▸ DAY 6

Part of what it means to live a relentless faith is that you share your faith in Christ with the world.

In light of this, we're going to devote Day 6 of each week to challenging you to do just that. Today, and the three remaining Day 6's, you're going to be presented with a verse. Your challenge is to take this verse and come up with some way to share it on Instagram or Snapchat or Vine. Be creative. Take a picture or video of something that comes to mind when you read this verse.

Have fun with this. And remember that sharing your faith journey with others is all part of leading people closer to Christ.

Here's your verse:

WEEK 1 ▸ DAY 7

Take Today Off... You've Earned it.

If you want, reflect on some of what you have learned. Look back and identify one day in the week that really stood out to you. What was it that was so meaningful? Dwell on this truth today. Think about the concepts of a relentless faith, true joy, and praising God in all situations. Listen for what God is trying to show you.

Looking Ahead

Here's a preview of what's coming up next week:

- **Week 2: Day 1 - Learning from 1 Peter 3:14-15, Part 1**
- **Week 2: Day 2 - Learning from 1 Peter 3:14-15, Part 2**
- **Week 2: Day 3 - A quote to make you think**
- **Week 2: Day 4 - What is your motivation?**
- **Week 2: Day 5 - A framework for sharing your faith**

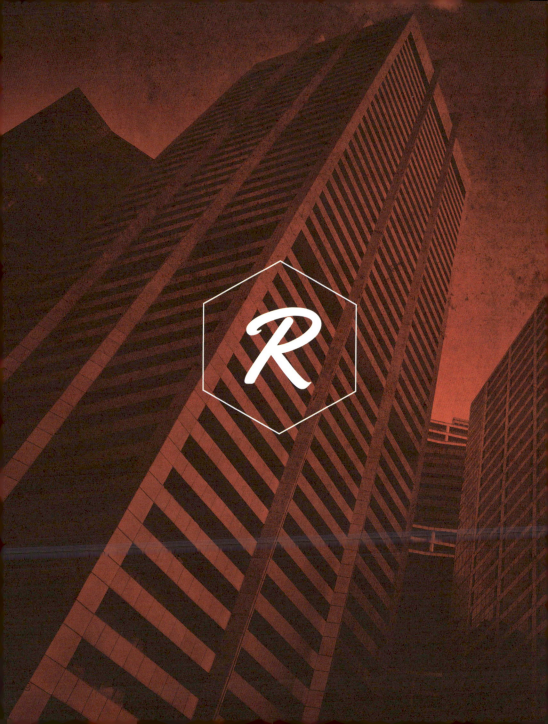

Week Two Intro

Before starting Week 2, read this short introduction.

What do you think when you hear the words, "personal evangelism"? For many people, it's the same feeling they get when they hear the words "personal fitness." Most people know that working out is good for them. And yet, there are a lot of people who don't actually live a fit lifestyle.

Sharing our faith is kind of like flossing. We know it's beneficial to us. We know it's a part of good overall health (in this case, a healthy faith). But we simply don't do it as often as we should.

But here's the part where we carve out space to talk about the way personal evangelism is different than working out or flossing or any other analogy. See, God never intended personal evangelism to be done in a grudging manner. God set up a system where His Kingdom would grow through the words of His children. He wanted us to be the best evidence of lives that were changed by His presence. And yet, if you were to survey Christians concerning the matter of sharing their faith story, there would be more than a little awkwardness. Why?

Christ-followers know the importance of sharing the good news of Jesus Christ concerning forgiveness, hope, and redemption. It's simply that many are uncertainty of the how, when, where, and what of sharing their faith.

How do we overcome the fear, the anxiety, and the challenge of obediently sharing our faith? How do we move from a faith that is timid in its expression to a faith that is relentless in seeing others come to know God?

This week's devotions won't have all the answers. But they'll get you started down the right path. Let's jump in to see what God can teach us about sharing our faith with the world around us.

WEEK 2 ▶ DAY 1

Read today's devotion below and answer the questions on page 24.

The thought of sharing your faith with others may cause you to feel a lot of emotions. It's an exciting, exhilarating act that draws you closer to God and to the person with whom you shared. But, for many Christ-followers, the thought of sharing their faith gives them more negative emotions than positive ones. Fear. Anxiety. Embarrassment. Maybe you're one of those people. But here's the deal: You don't have to be.

Take a moment and read 1 Peter 3:13-16. Read it carefully because we're going to spend the next two days looking at the takeaways from this passage.

1 Peter was written to Christ-followers who had been forced to spread throughout the Roman Empire because of persecution. Due to this persecution, the Christian community could no longer congregate in large numbers because they would be an easy target of hostility. Fear ran rampant. But Peter challenged these Christ-followers' cowardice. If anyone knew what it felt like to turn from his faith, it was Peter. Don't forget in Jesus' most trying moments, Peter not only denied Jesus, but also denounced Him. So, the feelings of shame and fear were battle scars Peter had already earned. But Jesus redeemed Peter and gave him a personal call to make Himself known to the world. This is the heart of 1 Peter!

Peter can stand up and emphatically say "Yes" to persecution, "Yes" to being marginalized, and "Yes" to being harassed and belittled! But most importantly, Peter could say "Yes" to being captured by grace, and to never wavering in a commitment to making God's love known.

So, what can we learn from Peter's teaching here? There will be four takeaways over the course of the next two days. Let's start our look at the first two by zooming in on 1 Peter 3:14-15. What we begin to see here is a framework for possessing a heart for personal evangelism.

Have No Fear.

The most prevalent reason why you probably don't share your faith in Christ isn't because you're not moved by your own salvation. Instead, there is one four-letter word keeping you from sharing: fear. Peter challenged his audience with a single motivational message concerning persecution: "Have no fear of them." (vs. 14)

Confession time: Have you ever been scared to share your faith? If you answered yes, why do you think you felt afraid? What were you afraid of?

If you truly believe that people who know Christ will be with Him in Heaven forever, and people who don't will be separated from Him for eternity, why would you fear someone's response?

What might you do to overcome your fear? Think about this question as you go through your day.

Honor God

In verse 15 Peter talks about honoring the Lord by setting Him apart as Lord. Jesus can't simply be another item on a priority list. Jesus must be your entire list. Period. Why is He worthy of such a position in your life? He is holy! When we set ourselves on the throne of our lives, death is our destination. However, with Christ as the center of our lives, our actions will reflect His mission.

In your own words, what does honoring God have to do with your effectiveness as someone who openly shares his or her faith?

Who is on the throne of your life right now? How does this impact your desire to share your faith?

If you're going to live a relentless faith, you must be willing to share it openly. Spend some time today meditating on these two truths. And get ready for two more truths tomorrow.

WEEK 2 ▶ DAY 2

Read the following devotion and answer the questions on page 26.

So, if you'll recall, yesterday we read from 1 Peter 3:13-16. We looked at two truths we can take from this passage as it relates to our personal call to share our faith with the world. What were these two truths?

Today we're going to examine the other two truths from this passage. Re-read 1 Peter 3:13-16. Then, look at the paragraphs below to learn the final two truths of this passage.

Give An Answer

vs. 15 says "Always be prepared to give an answer." How is this possible? When you seek Christ first in every facet of your life, then the natural result is to speak of what you seek. When you seek to know Christ the most natural response of your life will be to make Him known. This is where the phrase "give an answer" comes in (some of your Bible's may say "make a defense"). Some people may read confrontation into this. But this isn't the case. Instead, it's the understanding that the people you encounter on a daily basis are asking a question and you have the answer.

What is the question? Well, it takes on several different forms and fashions in its wording. But the core of the question is the same: "how can I find satisfaction in my life"? The endless pursuit of every person is to seek for something to satisfy his or her soul. How do we all share this in common? Easy! We were all created for eternity (Ecclesiastes 3:11). Therefore, since we were created by One who is eternal, and to live eternally prior to the curse of man, then our lives will never be satisfied until we are restored to harmony with our Creator. Because of your faith in Christ you were restored to the original intent of why you were created. Therefore, you have an answer to give the world. And that answer is Christ.

Think about a time when someone seemed to be asking the question, "How can I find meaning or satisfaction in my life"? How did you answer?

Would you answer them differently if you had to go back and do it over again?

Honor God

Peter encourages us to share Christ in "gentleness and respect." To share your faith this way is to exude humility. To walk in a deep concern for the people that God divinely brings into your life is to give them great value. The beauty of the earthly ministry of Jesus was most exemplified in His humility. He humbly came to this earth. He humbly served selflessly. He humbly gave value to the outcast. He humbly carried our sin to the cross of Calvary. He humbly died in our place. He humbly came back from the dead.

To have forgiveness and the hope of heaven could possibly cause one to walk in haughtiness or pride. But, if you want to live a relentless faith, you must instead embrace humility as Christ did. The free gift of salvation was afforded to humankind for a price we did not and could not pay. Therefore, it must be shared.

Define humility. Give a few examples about what it looks like in your context.

In your own words, what does humility have to do with sharing your faith?

How can pride keep you from doing the sometimes tough work of sharing your faith with those who need it most?

Here's the crazy thing: God has chosen to work through you. He didn't have to. But He did. He chose you to be His mouthpiece for spreading the news of the Gospel. Spend a few minutes today talking to God about this. Pray that your spirit would be moved to be more willing to jump on-board His mission to redeem people from their sins.

WEEK 2 ▸ DAY 3

Read the quote below and spend some time today thinking about it. Use the prompts on page 28 to help guide your thoughts.

"When our *Lord* sends us out to *witness for him,* he does not send us out against

A WALL

Rather, he gives us an *open door* for personal evangelism, an open door that *no man* can shut

- Josip Horak

Use these questions to help you reflect on this quote.

1. How does this quote make you feel? What is your first response to it?

2. Have you ever felt like you had a "closed door" when talking with someone about his or her faith? Horak was right: If God is all-powerful and intends a door to be opened, it will stay open! How might this truth give you hope when dealing with someone who may not seem at first to be open to conversations about faith?

3. Think about this today: How will you know if God has opened a door for you if you never try sharing your faith? You have to knock to know if it's open, right?

Spend some time in prayer that God would show you the opportunities He has opened for you. Pray that you would be relentless in your pursuit of those who most need to hear about God's love.

WEEK 2 ▸ DAY 4

So, we've talked about how sharing our faith is part of what it means to live a relentless faith. We've discussed some of the obstacles and the opportunities. But what we haven't talked about is the "why"?

Why do we share our faith?

The primary reason has to be that, because we love Jesus, we want to obey His commands. That's the main reason. But the second reason is a little more interesting. And maybe a little harder to arrive at. What is this motivation? Let's turn to Scripture to find our answer.

Read the account of Jesus in Matthew 9:35-38.

Jesus had just finished healing, and teaching, and performing miracles. In His own way, Jesus was sharing with the world what it meant that God had finally come to rescue people. Jesus was revealing the Kingdom of God to people, just like you do when you share your faith. But the coolest thing is that we see a bit of Jesus' motivation for wanting to save the people He encountered.

Vs. 36 says that when Jesus saw the people in need, people broken by sin, people lost apart from God . . . when He saw them, he had compassion over them. And in this moment, we see the answer to our secondary motivation for wanting to lead people to Jesus.

If we are to obediently embrace a life of sharing our faith, we must first discover compassion for the unredeemed. When was the last time you wondered if the person next to you had a relationship with Jesus? Have you paused long enough to ask the question if your classmate, friend, or teammate would spend eternity in heaven?

It's important to not see people as inconveniences or interruptions, but instead as divine opportunities God has given for the purpose of sharing Jesus. When you begin to see people the way God sees people, then you begin to look for opportunity. The desire to see someone come from death to life isn't born out of duty or obligation.

It's born out of love for God and love for others.

How would you define compassion? And what does it have to do with you sharing your faith?

Stop and think for a moment . . . List three or four people whom God has given you a sense of compassion for.

How many of these people don't have a saving relationship with Christ?

Are you willing to break through your fears and any social awkwardness to share your faith with this person? In the space below, write a prayer to God asking Him to give you the courage to share your faith boldly.

Compassion for the spiritually lost must drive your desire to share your faith. Pray that God would lead you to be more compassionate.

WEEK 2 ▸ DAY 5

When you find yourself ready to share your faith? What do you do? Read below for some helpful thoughts.

> *Those who had been scattered preached the word wherever they went.*
> *- Acts 8:4*

This verse from Acts describes the actions of the persecuted Christians who never stopped talking about Christ and what He had done in their lives. This is an example to us. This verse is kind of the theme verse for living out a relentless faith. We too should also be speaking of Jesus and the difference He has made in our lives wherever we go. But how do we do this? How do we think about going about sharing our faith?

The good news is that there is a framework we can use to begin thinking about how we talk about God's impact in our lives. Let's think about it in five parts.

Part 1
The first thing we can do to begin a conversation where we share our faith is to find a point of commonality. What can we discover in a brief moment of observation that can serve as a starting point of a conversation?

Part 2
The next thing we can do is to look for a way to transition the conversation in a spiritual direction. Think about asking a question like, "If you were to put a percentage on the chance that you will be in heaven after your life on earth ends, what percentage would you be? 50%? 100%? It is here that you are able to speak of the confidence you have in Christ and the peace you have in your soul as a result of your relationship with Him.

Part 3
Take the opportunity to speak of what Christ has done for you personally and then be willing to ask the person you are sharing with if they would like to have this same experience by giving their life to Jesus Christ.

Part 4

If they so desire to make this decision, then make sure they understand the following principles:

1. We are all Sinful (Romans 3:10, 3:23)

2. Christ died for Sinners (Romans 5:8)

3. Christ saves us from our Sin (Romans 10:9-10,13)

Part 5

Then lead them to ask Jesus, through prayer, to forgive them of their personal sin and become their Lord and Savior. It is here that it is important that you follow up with their decision in order to get them involved in a Christ-honoring and Bible-believing church.

So, do you think this is something you can do?

Spend some time in prayer today and over the next few days and weeks, asking God to reveal to you opportunities for you to share your faith with others using this framework. Trust that the Holy Spirit will work in and through you to plant the seed of faith in another person's life.

You can do it. God will help.

WEEK 2 ▸ DAY 6

As we've studied this week, part of living out a relentless faith is being excited about sharing your faith with those around you.

We're devoting Day 6 of each week to challenging you to embrace one aspect of a relentless faith. Like in Week 1, today you're going to be presented with a verse. Your challenge is to take this verse and come up with some way to share it on Twitter, Instagram, Snapchat or Vine. Be creative. Take a picture or video of something that comes to mind when you read this verse. Have fun with this. And remember that sharing your faith journey with others is all part of leading people closer to Christ.

Here's your verse:

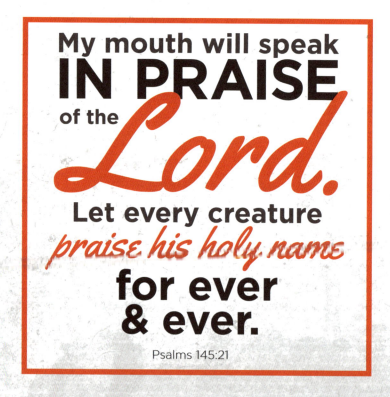

My mouth will speak IN PRAISE of the Lord. Let every creature praise his holy name for ever & ever.

Psalms 145:21

WEEK 2 ▸ DAY 7

Take Today Off... *Really, Take a Break.*

But don't stop thinking about God today. Don't stop listening to Him. Especially as He reminds you of those people who He's put in your life for a reason.

Look around you. Who in your life is committed to following Christ? Who do you see actively sharing God's story through their words and actions?

Thank God for him or her today.

Looking Ahead

Here's a preview of what's coming up next week:
- **Week 3: Day 1 - A devotion on the Lord's Prayer**
- **Week 3: Day 2 - The Three P's of the Lord's Prayer**
- **Week 3: Day 3 - The Three D's of the Lord's Prayer**
- **Week 3: Day 4 - Two quotes to make you think**
- **Week 3: Day 5 - Prayer: A 2-way Street**

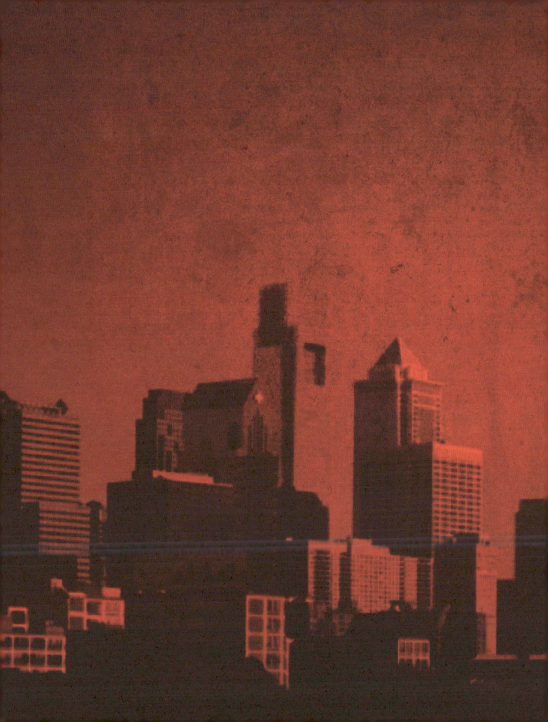

Week Three Intro

Before starting Week 3, read this short introduction.

It has been said that your generation of teenagers is the busiest generation to date. You are involved in more at any single time than any generation before you. Multitasking has become the norm, not the exception. You are busy. And when you're not busy you're flooded with media and messaging.

It's hard to focus on any one thing. In the midst of one conversation with someone there are to-do lists running through your mind. It's almost impossible to have a conversation without an interruption or a distraction. It is rare for anyone to give their undivided attention to a certain task, assignment, or conversation. Even as I type these very words I am listening to music.

So, how is someone to create sacred space and seek solitude with our Savior? Where in your life do you make room to talk to God? Where in your life do you make room to listen to God?

Jesus modeled what it looks like to carve out space to meet God in prayer. Jesus didn't have to answer emails, return phone calls, or post anything on Instagram. But He did have to deal with the overwhelming needs of people surrounding Him daily. In the chaos of daily lifestyles, it takes serious intentionality to find a quiet place and still one's heart before the Lord. The priority of being still before the Lord has become a lost art. And yet, it's only when you begin to pull back from the demands of life and truly wait before the Lord that deep intimacy begins to develop.

The next aspect of living a relentless faith is the aspect of prayer. To have a bold, authentic faith-life, you have to be grounded in prayer. That's what we're going to be looking at this week. Ready? Let's jump in.

WEEK 3 ▸ DAY 1

Read the following devotion and answer the questions on page 42.

Take a second today and read Matthew 6:5-13. This is Jesus' teaching on prayer that comes near the beginning of what is referred to as His Sermon on the Mount. It was sort of a collection of the ethical and moral expectations of God's people. It was revolutionary at the time, and is still so today, because of how it turns conventional wisdom on its head.

Smack in the middle of one of the greatest sermons ever preached, Jesus addressed the importance of prayer with those that had gathered that day on this hillside in Galilee. He went from speaking on the topic of generosity to prayer, and then back to generosity. What do you think He was trying to communicate with the positioning of prayer and generosity?

I think Jesus was trying to help us understand that a right view of prayer is one of "giving" verses "getting." See, the religious leaders of the day prayed simply to be noticed, to be applauded, and to receive. Now, don't misunderstand me; prayer is at its very core a request to receive from our Heavenly Father. However, when our prayers sound more like the seagulls off **Finding Nemo** (MINE, MINE, MINE!) then it's important that the selfish agenda of prayer be confronted. This is exactly what Jesus was doing here.

A person may claim dependence on the Lord in word and deed, but if the commitment to prayer is non-existent then there is a foundational challenge to the source of commitment. At the heart of prayer is the understanding that every believer faces a sense of inadequacy. With this transparency comes an understanding of dependency. This dependency leads each person to the request that the disciples made towards Jesus, which was, *"teach us how to pray."*

Think about the following questions. If you choose, write your answers down in the space provided.

1. How would you describe your prayer life? Healthy? In need of a little help? Non-existent?

2. The goal of prayer is not to simply fulfill a religious duty. The goal is to delight in meeting God in the language of our relationship. What is your attitude toward prayer? Do you see it as a delight or as a chore?

3. What changes can you make in your personal life to begin to get to a place where prayer becomes more important to you?

WEEK 3 ▸ DAY 2

What can we learn from the Lord's Prayer on how we should pray? Read the devotion below to find out.

There are a lot of ways we can look at what the Lord's Prayer has to teach us. Today and tomorrow, we'll look at two ways to dig-in and see what Jesus was trying to teach us.

We'll call them the three "P's" of the Lord's Prayer. Before we jump in, take a second and re-read Matthew 6:5-13. Finished? Good. Now for the first "P."

The Prohibitions of Prayer (Matthew 6:5, 7-8)

There are two prohibitions here. (Remember, a prohibition is basically a "do not do this.") The first is that Jesus prohibits us from trying to impress other people with our prayers. Jesus was speaking about groups of religious people who prayed to get noticed. Jesus said all they would receive was what they were looking for: getting noticed by others, not by God. God wouldn't honor their prayers because they weren't genuine. They only prayed the way they did to seem super-religious to those who could hear them.

The second prohibition is that we are prohibited from trying to impress God. Jesus warned us from trying to imitate the prayers of others. God doesn't need our big words. He doesn't need to hear us try to sound preachy. Why? Because God knows our hearts. He knows what we need before we know what we need. The last thing we should try to do is impress God with how we pray.

The Place of Prayer (Matthew 6:6)

Location was important to Jesus. We see Jesus oftentimes seeking out silence and solitude to meet God in prayer. Jesus said, "When you pray close your door." But wait a minute. Can't we pray anywhere? Yes! You never find Jesus going to a room and closing the door. He was oftentimes outside somewhere in the wilderness. So why did He say that we should go into a room?

The importance of the location is all about solitude. Jesus wanted us to focus on being separated from the distractions of life. Being alone is the best way to do that. "Close the door" is an often-overlooked phrase that could revolutionize not only your prayer life, but your life in general. Why? The moment you close the door to speak to the One who made the world, the world's distractions fade away.

The Pattern of Prayer (Matthew 6:9-13)

What if the challenge for you is what to say when you pray? If so, that's good. Because you're beginning to understand that prayer is more than just asking God for stuff.

Jesus did not give this prayer to us to be memorized and recited a given number of times. In fact, He gave this prayer to keep us from using vain repetitions. Jesus did not mean, "Pray these exact words." He meant, "Pray in this way." That is, "Use this prayer as a pattern, not as a substitute."

So what do you think? Do these three P's of prayer help you think about prayer in a different way?

The goal is not simply to get you to pray. Many people pray. The Hindu prays. The Buddhist prays. The Muslim prays.

The goal is not just to pray, but to connect with God when you do. The reward is the inner sense of peace THAT GOD SEES YOU and desires to communicate with you.

Take the time to pray today. Think about praying to God in an environment with no distractions. "Close the door." Make time to talk to and listen to God.

WEEK 3 ▸ DAY 3

Today you'll check out at one more way of looking at the Lord's Prayer and what it has to teach us.

The Lord's Prayer has a lot to teach us about HOW to pray. Yesterday we looked at the three "P's". Today we'll look at the three "D's."

Declare God's Glory:

When you pray, don't start with you. Start with God. Did you know the word "hallowed" translates to "great is your name"? When you start by declaring God's glory, you will get a better understanding of who you are and who you're dealing with. Ascribe worth and glory to God for who He is. Praise Him. Take as long as you need to properly worship Him. Get your heart around the idea that He is God. Stay on the subject of "hallowing" His name until it clicks and connects in your soul that God is simply greater than anything in your world!

Declaration of Surrender:

"Your kingdom come, your will be done on earth as it is in heaven." This is the aspect that you will wrestle with the most. A "kingdom" is a realm in which the will and power of a king are expressed. To pray God's "Kingdom come" is simply praying that God's agenda would come before your agenda. Your dreams, desires and demands fall at the will of your King. However, surrendering all of you to all of Him will never be a waste of your energy, time nor effort.

Declaration of Dependence:

The earth is sustained by the spoken Word of Jesus. Therefore, just as creation is dependent upon His provision, so must you be. Never take for granted that there is a personal God that you are privileged to call Father. He seeks to meet your needs. What an amazing thought!

There are three ways to think about declaring your dependence on God:

We declare the need for God's provision:
"Give us today our daily bread." The heart behind this request is the understanding that God seeks to meet our daily needs, much like He did with the nation of Israel in the wilderness journey where He rained manna from heaven. The lesson God desires for us to understand is not only that He provides, but that He sustains us each and every day.

Take time right now to thank God for providing all you see around you of His goodness.

We declare our need for a pardon:
"Forgive us our debts, as we also have forgiven our debtors." When we choose to sin it's a conscious choice to step out of fellowship with God. But it is God's kindness that leads us back to repentance. Asking God to forgive our debts is making the conscious choice to enter back into fellowship with God again. This same principle applies to our earthly relationships. When someone wrongs you and you make the choice to forgive him or her, you are making a choice to allow what has been done to no longer rule over you.

Who needs to be forgiven in your life today? Don't miss this chance to offer them grace.

We declare our need for God's Protection:
"And lead us not into temptation, but deliver us from the evil one." I like to use the phrase in my own life that "I am one step away from stupid every day of my life." I understand my selfishness, my pride, and my envy have the tendency to not only get in the way, but also blind me from the way. Our sin natures wage war against God and against us. Praying through this principle is asking God for this protection and insight on how to pursue righteousness. Seeking deliverance from evil serves as a convincing reminder that even though we have been forgiven we are to fight for holiness.

What does God need to deliver you from today? Pray and ask Him to lead you away from the dark places in your life.

WEEK 3 ▸ DAY 4

Read the quotes below and spend some time today thinking about them. Use the prompts on page 48 to help guide your thoughts.

"It is a *Good rule* never to look into the face of *man* in the morning until you have looked into the *face of God*"

— C. H. Spurgeon

"Do with your *Hearts* as you do with *your watches* wind them up every morning **by prayer** and at night examine whether your hearts have gone true all that day."

— Thomas Watson

Use these questions to help you reflect on these quotes.

1. What do both of these quotes have in common?

2. What about you? Do you normally start your day with prayer? What do you think the advantages may be to starting your day this way?

3. If you started every day talking and listening to God, how might it change the way you view the different obstacles and opportunities that you encounter through your day?

WEEK 3 ▸ DAY 5

Read the devotion below. Then, spend some time putting it into practice.

Prayer is not only a means in which people communicate with God. It's a two-way street. Prayer is also the way God communicates with people.

When an individual creates sacred space to hear from God, it is important not to begin with a list of requests, but instead approach prayer as a time of engaging with the one who already knows your needs and your requests before they even became apparent. God will reveal himself through prayer, if you're willing to pause long enough in solitude to hear from heaven.

When God chooses to speak to the human heart through prayer, He often brings to mind a verse, chapter, or passage of Scripture. When this happens, it's important to begin the process of digging-in to the Scriptures to see exactly what God is trying to show you.

It is an unspeakable privilege to be in a personal relationship with the God of the universe, who doesn't need humanity, but chooses to be actively involved in our lives. If you desire to be committed to godliness, if you want to truly live a relentless faith life, then you must recognize the value of listening to God, not just talking to Him.

Just as communication is the backbone of every relationship, so is prayer the backbone of your relationship with God.

Read the verse below:

BE
still
& know that
I am God

Psalm 46:10

Today, practice the discipline of listening to God.

Spend a few moments praising God in prayer.

Then, block out the distractions of the world and simply listen to God and what He might be showing you.

WEEK 3 ▶ DAY 6

Part of embracing a relentless faith is being bold in how you demonstrate your faith to the world.

Like in Weeks 1 and 2, today you're going to be presented with a verse. Your challenge is to take this verse and come up with some way to share it on Twitter, Instagram, Snapchat or Vine. Be creative. Take a picture or video of something that comes to mind when you read this verse. Have fun with this. And remember that sharing your faith journey with others is all part of leading people closer to Christ.

Here's your verse:

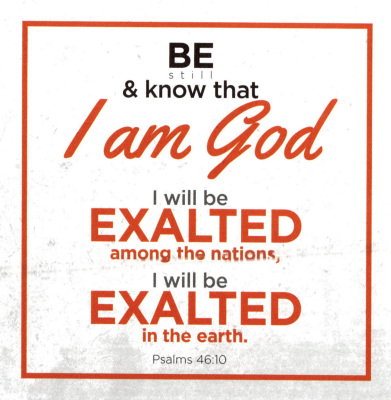

WEEK 3 ▸ DAY 7

Enjoy a Day Off... *and by enjoy it, we mean truly enjoy it.*

Take some time today and really soak in the world around you. See God in His creation. Thank Him for it. And praise Him by having as much fun today as you possibly can.

Here's a preview of what's coming up next week:
- **Week 4: Day 1 - An intro to persecution**
- **Week 4: Day 2 - Learning from Peter and John, Part 1**
- **Week 4: Day 3 - Learning from Peter and John, Part 2**
- **Week 4: Day 4 - A quote to make you think**
- **Week 4: Day 5 - A sign that your faith is strong**

Week Four Intro

Before starting Week 4, read this short introduction.

And so you're getting ready to wrap up this final week in this journal.

Good for you for sticking with it. That's actually pretty awesome.

You know, most people can't stick with something like this book for four weeks. And that's kind of sad, right? Our attention spans aren't even long enough for us to give God a few minutes a day for a month.

But if you're the kind of person who is still engaged with this journal, you're probably the kind of person who takes his or her relationship with God pretty seriously.

You're probably the kind of person who wants to live a relentless faith, no matter the cost.

Which is good. Because in this last section, we'll be talking about the cost of living your life as someone who publicly identifies with Christ. We'll take some time to talk about what living a relentless faith looks like and what may happen to you as a result. What you'll find is that, even though there are costs, there is no other way of living that gives you more than walking closely with God.

You're almost done with this book. Hang in there. This last week is a good one. You won't be disappointed.

Ready? Let's finish strong . . .

WEEK 4 ▸ DAY 1

Read the following devotion and answer the questions on page 60.

What do you think of when you hear the word persecution? It's kind of a big church word, isn't it? But if you're living your life as a Christ-follower, it's a word you've become familiar with probably (or definitely will). To be persecuted is to undergo any negative experience or outcome due to your faith in Christ. This looks a lot of different ways and can vary from context to context. But the point is this: if you are living a relentless faith, you will experience persecution. The Bible assures us of that over and over again.

Let's look at an early account of Peter and John experiencing persecution. Pay close attention as this account will be used for the next two days of Bible study.

Take a second and read Acts 4:12-20. Acts 3 opens up with an introduction to a man who had been born lame and sat on the "outside" of the temple gates begging. He was looked over day after day, unnoticed, overlooked and marginalized. However, this would change when he met Peter and John. Peter healed the man in the name of Christ! This was not well received by the religious leaders. The atmosphere became turbulent! Why? Not only did this contradict the religious message of the day—that salvation was by following more of the Law than you didn't follow—but it was proof that the power of Jesus changes everything.

The question that serves as the connector between Acts 3 and Acts 4 is this one question found in Acts 4:7: "By what power or what name did you do this"? See, religion is powerless, but the name of Jesus is powerful. It not only provided healing to a lame man, but empowered Peter and John to stand before the religious experts of the day and speak with boldness. The same group of men that were fearful for their lives behind a closed door because of the Pharisee's and Sadducees had gone from being cowards to courageous.

What are we supposed to take away from this passage?

First, because of their faith in Jesus, Peter and John experienced persecution. You will too.

They had not done anything wrong. In fact, they actually did something super compassionate. They healed a man. But because it was done in the name of Jesus, the were persecuted. You will find times in your life (maybe you already have) where you will be doing something positive but because you're doing it in the name of Christ, you'll be looked down upon. It's not fair. But it's true.

- Think of a time in your life when you experienced a negative outcome because you were doing something positive in the name of Christ. How did it make you feel?

Second, the presence of the Holy Spirit made Peter and John bold. It will make you bold too. And people may not like it.

Peter had a track record of running from tough situations. But the Peter in Acts is different than the Peter in the Gospels. The difference is the Holy Spirit. The presence of God in us will give us boldness and power we couldn't possibly have without Him. But, authentic faith causes discomfort in people who are threatened by it. Be prepared to have people question you and your motivation. But have no fear. You have God with you.

- Describe how Peter and John reacted to the religious leaders who opposed them. What can you learn from their response?

Spend some time in prayer today asking God to help you both be bold in your faith, but to also be gracious in how you respond to those who may come against you.

60

WEEK 4 ▶ DAY 2

Read today's devotion below to dig-in a little more on what we can take away from Peter and John's interaction in the Temple.

We're going to spend today and tomorrow digging a little deeper into the story of Peter and John. There's a lot to learn here, especially as it pertains to your living out a relentless faith.

Take a minute and re-read Acts 4:1-20, paying close attention to Acts 4:13-19. One thing we see about Peter and John is actually something we see in people who live a relentless faith. You see, Peter and John were marked by Christ.

Peter and John were being challenged not only because of their message, but also because of the manner in which they delivered it. There was an unusual power they spoke with. They had an authority about them that was noticeable. This power source isn't a force. But instead, it's a person. It's the Holy Spirit.

When you live in full surrender to the leadership of the Holy Spirit, your life will be marked with an unspeakable connection to the person of Jesus. It's the mark of the Christ in you. When Peter and John were accused of being "unschooled ordinary men" this wasn't just a criticism that they were un-educated. This was an understanding that they had not sat under an officially recognized rabbi. However, Jesus was their rabbi. And the lessons that they learned from Him made it very clear that they belonged to Him. They were marked as being in His presence.

What was this mark? What was it about them that made them different? Two things: They valued the people that their culture saw as un-valuable, and they spoke in power.

Peter and John showed love and compassion to man who was crippled. Why did they do this? Because Jesus had done this! They watched the Teacher and imitated what they learned.

Furthermore, what separated these disciples from all other rabbinical disciples was the fact they weren't just able to speak with authority, but were also able to demonstrate it by doing the miraculous things that Jesus did. This "bestowed power" was all made possible by the Holy Spirit at work in the heart of these disciples. So, when the religious leaders made the statement that Peter and John "were unschooled and untrained" one thing was evident: they had "been with Jesus," and that's all that mattered.

In the space below, write a few ways how you are able to practice "being with Jesus" in your life.

Think of some examples in your life of things you believe, or do, or hold valuable because Jesus did.

If someone were to look at your life, someone who didn't know you, would they see you as "marked" by Christ? Could they tell you spent time with Jesus regularly? How does your answer make you feel?

Make sure you spend some time in prayer reflecting on the difference Christ has made in your life and how this difference impacts those around you.

WEEK 4 ▶ DAY 3

You're going to wrap up your time in Acts 4 today. Read the devotion below to focus on your final lesson from Peter and John.

This will be our last look at what we can learn from Peter and John and their interaction with the religious leaders in the Temple. We've already talked about the persecution they faced for being identified with Jesus, and about how their words and actions marked them as followers of Christ. Today we'll look at one more aspect of their behavior.

Again, read back through Acts 4:1-20, paying close attention to Acts 4:20. Here, we see our last truth we'll be looking at: **Peter and John were motivated by conviction.**

Peter and John found themselves at a real crossroads. Peter had denied Jesus before. But this time, he would not make the same mistake again. As a matter of fact, when Peter and John were commanded to never speak in the name of Jesus ever again, Peter made it quite clear that their obedience is to the Lord and not man. However, there's an interesting statement that we should focus on. It gives us some insight into the conviction of these men, and what it took to not back down from persecution.

In Acts 4:20, Peter, once more filled with power from the Holy Spirit, makes a definitive statement that should grip our heart. He states, "we cannot help speaking about what we have seen and heard." Two questions must be asked, what did He see? And what did He hear? Simply, He saw the risen savior and he heard the words, "follow me." Let's explain.

The conviction that motivated these men to not back down and not waiver is founded in these two principles: "Christ is Risen and He has Forgiven"! Peter saw the resurrected Savior, which meant that everything Jesus told them was validated. What he heard was simply uttered to Peter in the midst of His shame and scandal of his denial. Between the initial "follow me" and the latter "follow me" is a statement of grace that covers a multitude of sin. Peter never got over this and made the mission of his life to never deny Jesus ever again, even if he was being threatened from the religious leaders of the day.

You know God. You know Him through the words of Scripture and through the presence of the Holy Spirit in your life. You experience Him in the words of other Christ-followers and through seeing the evidence of His hand in the world around you. Like Peter, you've been with Jesus. And like Peter, you have been changed by this. You stand up for your faith. You stay true to your convictions. This is what it means to live a relentless life.

> **Take a moment today and write in your own words how you are different because you know Jesus. Describe how you have the strength to stand up for your faith. And spend a moment talking about how having Jesus in your life gives you hope for the future.**

WEEK 4 ▸ DAY 4

Read the quote below and use the questions on page 66 to help you think about the quote as you go through your day.

Christ's followers CANNOT EXPECT better treatment in the world than their *Master had."*

- Matthew Henry

Use these questions to help you reflect on these quotes.

1. What does this quote mean to you?

2. We can be fooled into thinking that persecution is not something that Christians should experience. How does this quote remind us that this isn't the case?

3. If you experience persecution because of your relationship with Christ, what positive thing does that say about the way you live out your faith?

WEEK 4 ▸ DAY 5

Read today's devotion, then spend some time in prayer for the people around the world who are experiencing persecution.

Think about what you have read this week.

The implications of this week are simple: being a Christ follower is costly. To receive salvation is easy. God is awesome in that way. However, responding to the gift that you've received in your salvation is what is challenging. See, you aren't seeking to be obedient to God to earn your salvation. That's already been done for you. You obey God, and thus set yourself up for persecution, because you are saved! This is where it gets costly.

To seek to honor Jesus with your life will cause you to brush against the grain of society, causing friction. How you handle these moments of persecution reveals a lot about how you view God. If you think God is out to make you suffer, then you view God is a tyrant and un-loving. I want to challenge you from this perspective: don't view your current difficulties, challenges or persecutions as evidence that God doesn't love you. Because quite the opposite is true. God loves you so much that He gave you Jesus. And suffering on this earth for the namesake of Christ is the greatest privilege ever.

To be despised or rejected means that you're carrying on the work of Jesus and clashing with the worldly culture you find yourself surrounded by. Don't think for a moment that Christianity is for the faint of heart. The challenge of living your life as a credit to Jesus while everyone else seeks to curse Jesus will be discouraging at times. Yes, you won't be invited to the parties anymore, or people will even talk different around you. There might even be a moment that you get tired of being treated so different, but don't ever forget this: You were never called to blend in, but to stand out.

Never take it as a criticism that you are being persecuted, instead take it as a compliment that your life has been so closely identified with Christ that you find yourself suffering as He did. Why would this be a compliment? Your life committed to things of Christ has the ability to change eternity forever and rightfully do great damage to Satan himself. As he seeks to steal, kill and destroy, you are overthrowing and conquering in the name of Jesus. What a privilege to be persecuted for the sake of Jesus and fellowship with His suffering.

Take a few moments today and simply pray for those in this world experiencing suffering and persecution for the sake of Christ. Pray that they would be lifted up by God and strengthened by the Holy Spirit. Pray that God would lead you to be faithful in staying strong in how you represent Him regardless of what comes your way.

WEEK 4 ▸ DAY 6

Living a relentless faith life is all about shining your light brightly in the world around you. Day 6 of this week is a challenge to do just that.

Your challenge is to take this verse and come up with some way to share it on Twitter, Instagram, Snapchat, Vine. Be creative. Take a picture or video of something that comes to mind when you read this verse. Have fun with this. And remember that sharing your faith journey with others is all part of leading people closer to Christ.

Here's your verse:

WEEK 4 ▶ DAY 7

As Usual...
this day is on the lighter side.

But, you have one task for today. Somewhere in the bottom part of this page, summarize what you've learned over the past four weeks in one sentence.

Think about this concept as you go through the next couple of days. Consider how it has impacted your understanding of faith.

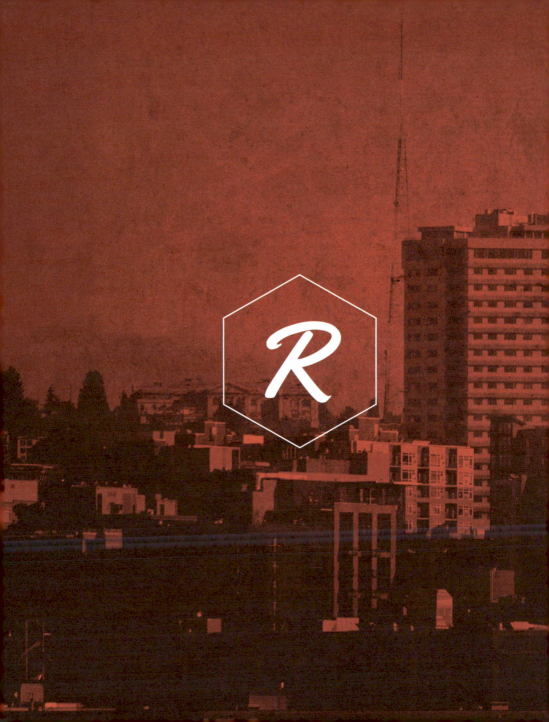

Wrapping Up

And so you've reached the end of your four weeks of working through this journal. It's really awesome that you made it this far. Hopefully it has been a worthwhile experience for you.

But there is a very real question that's worth asking: Will you live a relentless faith life? Will you praise God regardless of circumstances? Will you seek to know Him more in prayer? Will you take persecution in stride, staying true to God and to your convictions?

Your challenge is to get serious about the kind of faith you're living. Your relationship with God isn't one thing among many aspects of your life. It should define your life in a way that nothing else even comes close. The call of every Christian is to pursue God with all that they have. You can do this. And if you do, the world will be changed as a result.

Don't let this chance to make real life change pass you by. Do whatever it takes to make a change in your life.

Embrace the kind of faith Jesus died to earn for you. Don't settle for anything less than a relentless desire to know Jesus and make Him known to the world.

About the Author

Few speak and teach the Word with as much passion and clarity as Ed Newton. Ed travels the country sharing about the truth of Christ that he found while living through difficult circumstances and major hardships in high school. As the only child of two deaf parents, Ed lived in a world of silence. In those early days, it was through the spoken word of others and the written Word of God that clarified a call to ministry as a senior in high school. God began to show forth His sovereign will in leading Ed to Clearwater Christian College to gain a Biblical education, while affording the opportunity to play college basketball for four years. Ed continued his education journey by receiving a Master in Religious Education from Mid-America Baptist Theological Seminary, a Master of Divinity from Trinity Theological Seminary, and a Doctorate of Ministry from Trinity Theological Seminary. Ed has served on church staffs as Youth Minister, Rec Pastor, Minister of Outreach and Single Adults, Staff Evangelist and other teaching roles. Additionally, his ministry has served alongside countless churches and national ministries. His communication style can be summarized as "passion with content" while seeking to inspire people to be passionate, dedicated followers of Christ. He and his wife Stephanie, and their four children London, Liv, Lola and Lawson live out the call daily to make disciples as a family on mission.

WHAT IF THERE WERE A RESOURCE TO HELP YOU TAKE OWNERSHIP OF YOUR FAITH?

WELL, NOW THERE IS.

Introducing "NEXT," the 4-week devotional journal that helps challenge and equip you to take ownership of growing deeper in your faith.

THE PERFECT FOLLOW-UP TO "NEW: FIRST STEPS FOR CHRIST-FOLLOWERS."

"NEXT" WILL TEACH YOU...
- Why it's important to own your faith
- What your life's purpose has to do with God's missions
- How to build spiritual habits that last a lifetime
- How to use the influence you already have for Christ

TO VIEW SAMPLES OF NEXT & TO ORDER,
GO TO YM360.COM/NEXT

DO YOU KNOW THE STORY OF THE BIBLE?

Better yet, did you even know it WAS a story? The Bible is an awesome story! Tracing The Thread is a daily devotion that can help you learn the big-picture story of God's Word. More than that, it will help you trace the thread of the Gospel through the narrative of Scripture.

WANT TO KNOW MORE ABOUT TRACING THE THREAD?
CHECK OUT **YM360.COM/THREAD-DEVO** FOR SAMPLES & ORDERING INFO.